I0492698

RECRUITER SECRETS

What recruiters want you to
know, but don't tell you

DANIELLE GRUPPO

Copyright © 2018 Danielle Gruppo

All rights reserved.

ISBN: 9781723713828

DEDICATION

To Sean,
Life partner, best friend, my most supportive person

To Mom and Dad,
Who taught me at an early age
that I could do anything

.

CONTENTS

INTRODUCTION

In this practical and lighthearted guide, Danielle Gruppo reveals what only insiders know about navigating the job search and interviewing process to become a top candidate for hire.

Recruiter Secrets has been designed to answer your job search questions and concerns in a concise and easy to read manner. This book is for people who suffer from job search, interview anxiety, and are new to or overwhelmed by the process.

Anyone privileged in choosing their career path is cursed with a common burden…job search and interviewing. Whether you're a student, recent graduate, or even someone making a mid-career move, knowing how to navigate the rough waters could make or break your career.

> ➢ Knowing that you are fully qualified for the job, have you ever envisioned your application stuck in a black hole?
>
> ➢ Following an application submission or interview, have you ever wondered if you presented yourself correctly or could have done better?

Both of these unknowns cause anxiety, which undoubtedly add to the probability of a negative outcome in your job search process.

Drawing examples from her time as chief executive officer of the social recruiting platform InternAlliance, talent management, diversity and inclusion strategist, AND over 25 years of coaching professionals through their career progression, Gruppo shows the reader how to put their best foot forward in getting the job they deserve.

The insights you're about to read have been proven to create positive results. **All you need to do to stay in control of your career search is to keep reading.** Each chapter will give you new tips as you endeavor to get the job you deserve.

Learn recruiter secrets to get the job you want.

ACKNOWLEDGMENTS

My continuing source of material are those thousands of human resources, business, career services professionals, and college students in my social networks who provide unfiltered input and feedback to keep my content modern and useful. There are many who have contributed their perspectives, several of which made it into this book. Amy Soricelli – Vice President Career Services Berkeley College, Sharon Castano – Director of Internships Wilkes University, Tracey Hanton – Career Connections Specialist Community College of Philadelphia, Anne - Assistant Professor Purdue University, Heather Krasna – Assistant Dean Career Services Columbia University School of Public Health, Amy Blythe – Assistant Director Lafayette College, Tomomi C. Uetani – Director Career Services and Leadership Management Columbia School of Social Work, Dwayne Keiffer – Assistant Director Messiah College, Nora Newhouse – Human Resources Generalist-Benefits PMH Medical Center, Christy Decker – Human Resources Manager D.D. Williamson, Bonnie Turner – Director, Human Resources Elkhart Plastics Inc., Amanda – Recruiter CSRA, Hannah Smith – Recruiter Conagra Brands, Ken Kuwamura – Director of Employee Relations Union Pacific, Noelle Keeler – Senior Human Resources Generalist Lehigh Cement Company, LLC, Raphael Oritz – student Political Science Columbia University, Carmelo Rivera – student Business Administration Capella University, Brooke Stone – student Marketing University of Scranton, Larissa Schneck – student Business

Administration Bloomsburg University.

To my close network of friends and colleagues - I appreciate your support, contributions, and encouragement. I am grateful to all of those who have contributed to thoughtful and insightful discussions.

Specific contributors for this book include Lucille Gruppo - Editor, Concetta O'Leary, and Erin O'Leary.

1

FUNNY, NOT

*When you're not concerned with succeeding,
you can work with complete freedom.*

~ Larry David

~

Flirting with the
interviewer won't
get you the job,
or a date.

~

Your interviewers are not your friends, be cautious of being overly familiar.

~

Be polite to everyone you meet, especially the receptionist.

~

Ghosting is bad—No call/no show to an interview ruins any chance of future employment with that company and other companies in the recruiters' network.

~

Bashing prior
employers
doesn't make a
good impression.

~

Sometimes jobs are advertised although there is a strong chance an internal candidate will fill the job—This is done more often than you think.

~

When you blow
your first
impression, you
won't be given
the opportunity
to make a second
one.

~

There is a really good chance that a recruiter will ask mutual connections for a reference—Get ahead of the game by giving those colleagues insights they can use.

~

Interacting with recruiters face-to-face is becoming a lost skill— Practice makes perfect.

~

One or two internships under your belt will set you a head and shoulders above the rest for entry-level opportunities.

~

Some companies are perceived as lacking an inclusive culture—If inclusion and diversity are important to you, do your research before accepting an offer.

2

VIGILANCE

An owl is traditionally a symbol of wisdom, so we are neither doves nor hawks but owls, and we are vigilant when others are resting

~ Urjit Patel

~

Create more than
one resume if
your skills
support multiple
career paths—
Make sure you
submit the right
one when
applying.

~

Tailor your
resume and cover
letter to reflect
key words used in
the job posting—
Recruiters search
on keywords.

~

Most recruiters
have a time-to-fill
goal metric—
Simplifying your
application
submissions
makes it easier to
get from point A
to B for them
and you.

~

Ten minutes early is late for an interview.

~

Research the company prior to your interview— Become familiar with the executive team, the business lines, and the latest news.

~

Be prepared to
ask one to three
intelligent
questions that
can't be found on
the company
website.

~

Discounting the
recruiter when
you meet the
hiring manager is
a mistake you will
regret—They
recommend who
to hire.

~

Keep records of where you have applied and notes on correspondence —You don't want to mix up your conversations.

~

Own your past
work experience
by describing
what you did to
grow and
improve yourself
or the
company—i.e.
saved company
money, improved
efficiencies.

~

Prepare to respond to interview questions with real work/life scenarios—A web search will uncover free behavior-based questions for any career.

~

Jotting down key words and phrases to glance at during the interview helps you verbalize examples or tell a story.

~

Each candidate
has unique
motivators that
drive them to
choose one
company over
another—Make a
list and focus on
your top five.

~

Company values
are not always the
ones written on a
website—Ensure
they are evident
in the culture.

~

Each job posting
receives hundreds
of applicants—
Recruiters filter
by most qualified
and scan twenty
to fifty at a time
until they have a
good candidate
pool for
interviewing.

3

DRESS THE PART

*Age and size are only numbers. It's the attitude
you bring to clothes that make the difference.*

~ Donna Karan

~

When a recruiter recommends that you dress professionally for the interview, ask for clarification and follow their direction.

~

'Business casual'
is not standard
across
companies—In
most cases it
means khakis,
tucked in golf
shirt or blouse,
and dress shoes.

~

It is better to
over dress than
under dress—
You can always
take layers off,
but a jacket won't
simply appear.

~

If the industry you are interviewing for is a work casual environment, candidates should dress one step up for an interview.

~

If a typical workday is t-shirt and jeans, interviewees should wear khakis and a golf shirt or blouse— No jacket or tie required.

~

Wardrobe doesn't have to be muted—Add color with a smart top and accessories.

~

Many hiring managers are under the belief that you should come dressed to impress for an interview, demonstrating you want the job—Their opinion counts.

~

An unkept look
won't impress the
interview team.

~

Test your
neckline by
moving around—
Being able to see
your bra, chest
hair, or belly
button is your
clue to change.

~

Wear closed toe
shoes to the
interview—Even
in a warm climate
there is air
conditioning.

~

Iron or dry-clean
your khakis and
button-down
shirt or blouse—
Tuck it in and
wear a belt.

~

A blue, gray, or black suit jacket is a good choice—You can express your personal brand once you get the job.

~

Cover your
tattoos with a
long sleeve
shirt—Or the
focus with be on
your art not your
skills.

~

Your belt should match your shoe color.

~

Remove visible
piercings—
Tongue and nose
rings will shift the
conversation
away from the
interview.

~

Get a haircut and
ensure your hair
is well
groomed—First
impressions can
make or break
you.

~

Men with long hair should pull it into a short pony tail or bun—not necessarily a *Game of Thrones* Dothraki one.[1]

---

1 Benioff, D. and Weiss, D. (2015)."Winter Is Coming." *Game of Thrones (TV Series 2011–)* HBO. 17 April 2011.

4

PERSONAL BRAND

People should pursue what they're passionate about. That will make them happier than pretty much anything else.

~ Elon Musk

~

Prepare a 30 second elevator pitch to say anytime you are in the presence of an influencer— Use pitch also to kick off your interview.

~

Have a firm handshake—It sets the tone for the rest of the interview.

~

Strong people are always afraid of hurting the hand they shake—You won't, so don't shake with a limp wrist.

~

Be authentic and
memorable—
Stand out in a
good way.

~

Smokers are
perceived as
taking a lot of
breaks to feed
their habit—
Reeking of
smoke in the
interview makes
an unreliable
impression.

~

Think about who
you are and how
you want to be
perceived—This
may change
slightly for each
career
opportunity.

~

Be engaging on
the phone and in
person—Smiling
and sitting up
straight usually
sets a positive
tone.

~

One good reason
to attend a job
fair; your
company of
choice is
attending, and
you want face
time to build
your personal
brand.

~

Tell **your story** when asked for examples—**It is only yours to tell**.

~

A key to
successful
networking; find
a commonality
with everyone
you meet.

~

When writing
your thank you
note, integrate a
few relevant
commonalities
you identified
with the
interviewer.

~

Integrate your values into the conversation, not just skills and competencies.

DANIELLE GRUPPO

5

FOOT TO MOUTH

I love Cee Lo, but I avoid him when he's holding that smelly cat.

~ Blake Shelton

~

Take a shower
the day of the
interview—It will
wake you up and
get your creative
thoughts flowing.

~

Lick your wrist
and smell it—If it
stinks so does
your breath.

~

Bad breath will shut down a stellar interview quickly—Bring breath mints.

~

Sweaty hands are gross—Wipe your palms off before shaking hands.

~

Body odor in close quarters is game changing and not for the better—Use deodorant.

~

Your feet will be directly under the interviewers' nose—Add a touch of baby powder in your shoes before putting them on.

DANIELLE GRUPPO

6

GOOD CHOICES

What you know today can affect what you do tomorrow. But what you know today cannot affect what you did yesterday.

~ Condoleezza Rice

~

Answer online application pre-screening questions—Correct answers will put your resume in the qualified pile.

~

After making it
through the initial
automated pre-
screening
process, your
resume is the first
impression.

~

A successful
initial phone
screen is key to
getting invited to
a face-to-face
interview.

~

Many recruiters favor qualified candidates whose school or home address is in close proximity to their company location.

~

Have a conversation with each recruiter— Making a connection will ensure they remember you for current and future opportunities.

~

Make eye contact
with all the
interviewers, not
just the hiring
manager or
recruiter.

~

Interview the company as much as they are interviewing you—Culture fit goes both ways.

~

The initial salary
offer is rarely as
high as the
recruiter will go,
so negotiate—
The worst they
can say is no.

~

There are particular benefits that are fairly cheap for the company to provide—
Flextime, vacation, and a sign on bonus are all negotiable.

~

With two jobs being equal, additional factors to deliberate are pay, proximity to home or paid relocation, and growth potential.

~

Some decision
points to
consider before
accepting an
offer: The
company status
in the
community, and
do you believe in
their product or
service.

7

LEGALITIES

There should be no discrimination against languages people speak, skin color, or religion.

~ Malala Yousafzai

~

Completing the self-identification questions in an online application will only improve your chances of being hired into an inclusive company—Don't include that information anywhere else.

~

The United States government requires companies with affirmative action plans to actively recruit and track diverse applicants—This includes race, gender, veteran status, and disability.

~

Companies love
veterans—
Veterans are a
gateway group
for companies to
build a culture of
diversity and
inclusion.

~

Companies with affirmative action plans must prove their outreach and sourcing is **effective** in attracting qualified, diverse applicants—The operative word is **'effective'**.

~

Statistically speaking, effective diversity outreach equals an increase in diversity hires— The results are not typically shared beyond company leadership and government reporting.

~

If a recruiter's candidate pool produces a hire, other qualified resumes that weren't reviewed, will never be.

~

Most companies
don't inquire
about LGBTQIA
in the application
process, rather
after employment
via inclusion
surveys.

~

Being deceitful in the interview process will only waste the time of the hiring team— A background check will prevent you from getting in the door.

~

Some job postings have thousands of applicants, yet recruiters complain of not having the right ones—Save time and only apply if you've met the basic qualifications.

~

Basic job
qualifications
must be met
when applying, or
the recruiter will
never see your
application.

~

Meeting the basic <u>and</u> preferred requirements of the job will put you in a higher priority during the candidate review process.

~

Many hiring managers don't recognize the difference between compliance and diversity inclusion— Canvass the company culture before you agree to work there.

~

Applicants will make it to candidate status once their resume is reviewed.

~

Volunteering your political, religious, or marital affiliations should take full consideration— Interviewers cannot ask you outright.

~

Many recruiters toss legal advice into the wind and will search your name online as part of an 'unofficial' background check.

8

DIFFERENTLY ABLED

However difficult life may seem, there is always something you can do and succeed at.

~ Stephen Hawking

~

Many employers
are required to
actively source
qualified, disabled
applicants—
Measuring
outreach and
hiring goals are
required.

~

Application system accessibility is apparent when on a website—A posted accessibility report and closed caption videos are good first clues.

~

Voluntarily submit your disability status **only** on the self-identification form online— This ensures the hiring team does not see it.

~

The United States government has an expanded disability definition for applicants and employees that include diabetics, cancer survivors, and PTSD.

~

Ask for a reasonable accommodation as soon as possible—
Having a recruiter scramble to accommodate you will leave a lasting impression **you do not want**.

~

Don't share your disability with the hiring team—It's none of their business.

~

Having a visible disability will be open to performance questions—Many recruiters will imagine how you will perform.

~

Some
interviewers are
uncomfortable
around the
disabled, or
anyone else that
is different from
them—Exude
positivity and be
yourself.

~

Recruiting teams consider physical and mental disabilities when determining job qualifications— **It's up to you to prove your worth.**

~

An inclusionary
culture embraces
the disabled—
Investigate
before accepting
a position.

9

SOCIAL CODE

Innovation distinguishes between a leader and a follower.

~ Steve Jobs

~

Your resume
should match
your professional
LinkedIn
profile—Yes, you
should have one.

~

Create a LinkedIn profile and connect to people in your field of interest, even if you don't know them.

~

Comments and posts on social media, blogs, and forums never go away.

~

While job searching, answer unknown callers or the next candidate will.

~

Fun and catchy profile names and emails are for personal use only—Create a separate email for the application process.

~

Text messages shouldn't look like text messages.

~

Using text shortcuts when responding to a recruiter's correspondence denotes immaturity and lack of professionalism.

~

Keeping your sweetheart's voicemails are touching, but if you want a job, make space for the recruiters.

~

You may be a top candidate today, but not tomorrow if you don't return calls promptly.

~

Put your
electronics on 'do
not disturb' while
speaking to a
recruiter on the
phone or face to
face.

~

Go old school by
using pen and
paper during an
interview—Using
electronics to
take notes is
distracting.

10

INTERNATIONAL

Never bend your head. Always hold it high.
Look the world straight in the eye.

~ Helen Keller

~

Getting a job
while possessing
a student or work
visa gets you
experience and
the employer
your expertise—
Not a bad gig.

~

International applicants are infrequently considered for long-term hire— The exception is for those that possess rare in-demand skills.

~

The United States government caps the number of H-1B work visas distributed each year; limiting corporate sponsorship to science, engineering, and information technology employees.

~

F-1 and M-1 student visas have limitations to off campus employment— Know your visa employment facts.

~

Companies seldom invest in the high cost of hiring and training international interns or recent graduates with common skill sets and visas, only to see them leave in a few years.

~

Pre-screening application questions are carefully scripted to identify applicants authorized to work in the United States and are non-discriminatory when worded properly.

DANIELLE GRUPPO

ABOUT THE AUTHOR

Danielle Gruppo is chief executive officer and founder of InternAlliance—a consulting firm and social recruiting platform bridging the gap between education and employment for student interns and campus brand ambassadors, while strengthening the workforce pipeline for top employers.

Ms. Gruppo is an accomplished human resources executive with over 25 years of experience developing and executing talent management and human capital strategies for Fortune 250 and privately held companies in energy, healthcare, services, and manufacturing. Gruppo is adept at leading comprehensive organizational design, long-term recruiting and retention strategies, workforce development, global diversity/inclusion strategy and creating human resources frameworks in support of companies' overall goals and values.

Ms. Gruppo is a sought-after speaker who provides insights and practical tools for increasing job search success. Connect with Danielle Gruppo via LinkedIn and invite her to speak at your campus, work event, or conference by visiting www.InternAlliance.com.

www.ingramcontent.com/pod-product-compliance
Lightning Source LLC
Chambersburg PA
CBHW051316220526
45468CB00004B/1375